SO-CPE-969

Sharing Time

By J. A. Vezzetti

Illlustrated by Jacqueline Decker

"We all have special things about us,"
Miss Benson tells the children. "Thursday you will
all share something about you that is special."

The children think about what they should
share. They all have different ideas. But they have
one idea in common. Each one wants to share
something that the class will like best.

Joe cannot decide what to share. He looks at the pennies he has collected. They fill several boxes. His classmates might gasp at the hundreds and hundreds of pennies.

Or he could take the reptile skin he found on a hike. Which thing should he choose?

Lisa looks around her room. She knows there are many things that make her different. But she doesn't know what to take to class. Should she take the trombone her dad gave her? the baskets she wove at camp? Which object will her classmates admire most? Lisa rethinks her ideas.

Eric likes making people laugh. He could tell his classmates a funny tale. Last week Eric tripped. His glasses fell off and landed on his dog's nose. Everybody would laugh at that.

But Eric decides to bring his new trumpet. He has only had one lesson on it. He hopes his classmates don't laugh at him when he plays it.

Hannah thinks. She could show her classmates the rug she is making. But it is incomplete. She could take her fossil bone. But she does not know much about it.

Hannah thinks some more. Everybody knows that she loves ants and wasps. But they don't know that she has an ant farm.

Hannah discusses the idea with her mom.

In class the next morning Miss Benson hears the children discuss their desire to share the best thing. She dislikes this idea.

"Class," she says. Everybody stops to listen.

"This is not a contest to win. It is about connecting with one another. It is about sharing something about ourselves. Then we can see how we are alike and different."

"Let's work together," Lisa says to Eric. "Our classmates will hear what we can do with our trumpet and trombone."

"Great!" says Eric.

"Let's work together," Joe says to Hannah. "We will tell others why we like to collect things."

"I can't wait to show everybody my ant farm!" says Hannah.

Miss Benson smiles as the children discuss their plans.